BRINGING OUT THE BEST IN YOUR EMPLOYEES

*The Ultimate Guide for Managers and Supervisors
for Engaging and Empowering Employees
to Be More Successful and Productive
Through Effective Communication*

BRINGING OUT
THE BEST
IN YOUR EMPLOYEES

The Ultimate Guide for Managers and Supervisors
for Engaging and Empowering Employees
to Be More Successful and Productive
Through Effective Communication

Lisa Giruzzi

Design Credits:

Cover Design
KillerCovers.com

Photo of Author
Joan Heffler | www.joanheffler.com

Book Published By
CreateSpace

Book sales contact:
Lisa@YourCommunicationAuthority.com
888-330-8288

ISBN: 1456450492
ISBN-13: 9781456450496

Disclaimer: The purpose of this book is to educate and entertain. The author or publisher does not guarantee that anyone following the techniques, suggestions, tips, ideas, or strategies will achieve success. The author and publisher shall have neither liability nor responsibility to anyone with respect to any loss or damage caused, or alleged to be caused, directly or indirectly by the information contained in this guide.

"The most important thing in communication is to hear what isn't being said."

Peter Drucker

American (Austrian-born) management writer (1909–2005)

Acknowledgments

"There is no such thing as a 'self-made' man. We are made up of thousands of others. Everyone who has ever done a kind deed for us, or spoken one word of encouragement to us, has entered into the make-up of our character and of our thoughts, as well as our success."

~George Burton Adams
(1851–1925) Educator, Historian

First and foremost I want to acknowledge and thank my husband, Bill Giruzzi, for the huge contribution he has made not only to this book but also to my life. To say my husband is extraordinary would be an understatement. He is brilliant in so many ways, not the least of which is in his ability to communicate and cause transformation. I adore and admire you.

Thank you to my clients, who have amazed and inspired me by their willingness to engage in a discovery process with me to forge new pathways and achieve their desired outcomes. It has been a privilege to work with each and every one of you and learn with you how to create an environment that brings out the best in people. I am forever grateful.

To my colleagues and friends who have allowed me to share my ideas with them and who have been so eager to share their ideas with me to make this book a reality, I thank you with all my heart.

Introduction

It is time to recognize the awesome power of communication and its capacity to transform your world. The traditional definition of "communication" is narrow and mostly limited to speaking and listening, reading and writing, verbal and nonverbal.

> **com·mu·ni·ca·tion (kə-myōō'nĭ-kā'shən) n.** The act of communicating; transmission. The exchange of thoughts, messages, or information, as by speech, signals, writing, or behavior. Interpersonal rapport. The art and technique of using words effectively to impart information or ideas.[1]

In reality, communication is far more encompassing than that. We communicate and receive communication through everything we experience. Our mind is constantly interpreting what we are experiencing. It is constantly making meaning of the world it sees. Consequently, everything is in the realm of communication.

Someone cuts you off in traffic—that communicates something. The cashier smiles at you; that's a communication. You promise to exercise and you do or you don't; both are communications. Your significant other doesn't call when he or she is supposed to; that's communicating something. You oversleep and miss a big meeting; that is a communication. Your employee is late; he or she is telling you something. Every time you perceive the world, it is communication.

This book (and all my work) uses the broadest possible definition of "communication." When you understand communication in this way, you get a glimpse of the vastness of the topic and, more importantly, the magnitude of its impact.

Communication is everything and everything is communication. For human beings there is nothing that exists in the world without it. If it does, it is outside our ability to understand or perceive it and therefore it doesn't exist *to us.*

This book is subtitled *The Ultimate Guide* because it will expand your definition of communication and increase your awareness of your communication in every minute of every day in many, many ways, most of which until now have been unconscious. In this book you will discover the many facets of communication, allowing you to enhance your ability to engage and empower your employees to be more successful and productive.

---

1   1. *American Heritage Dictionary of the English Language,* 4th ed. (Boston: Houghton Mifflin Company, 2004). http://dictionary.reference.com/browse/communication (accessed March 14, 2010).

How to get the most out of this book

Read it with an open mind. Many of the concepts introduced in this book are counter to the traditional management/supervisor approach to communication. Have you noticed the traditional approach is not working to bring out the best in your employees?

This is not a "how to" book in the traditional sense. This book is designed to challenge your thinking, which will lead to new and more effective ways of communicating, which will lead to, as the book's title states, *Bringing Out the Best in Your Employees.*

After each topic, there is a page designed to get you involved in the conversation. The opportunity of these pages is to give you a place to reflect on the ideas put forth in this book and to declare how you will implement them. Use these pages to enhance your experience of the book and to have the concepts make a real, measurable difference in your reality.

The first step to change is to shift your thinking. The next step is to take new actions consistent with the new thinking. That is where the "rubber meets the road," so to speak. If you want different results, you have to think something new.

To benefit from this (or any) book, you must allow the new thinking to influence your actions. Take the time to think through how these ideas can change you so you can, in turn, bring out the best in your employees!

Keep this book on your desk at work, and when you are faced with a challenge, open randomly to a particular topic, read it, and think about the topic in relationship to the challenge you are dealing with. This will expand your thinking and help you to deal with the challenge more effectively.

Let the journey begin!

Note: The words *manager* and *supervisor* are used interchangeably throughout this book.

Effective Communication Begins with Attitude

When you understand that communication is a far broader topic then merely speaking, listening, writing, reading, and verbal and nonverbal exchanges; when you recognize that communication is happening in every moment because we are always making meaning; then you can see the significance of this assertion: effective communication begins with attitude.

Our attitude does more than shape what we say out loud; it shapes how we interpret the world. This goes beyond a positive or negative point of view or glass-half-full kind of stuff. It includes that, but really is more expansive. This is about the attitudes and beliefs we have developed over time, the ones that are so deeply embedded in our thinking that we don't even question them. Put simply, it's how we see the world. We forget that it is just *our* perspective, and then we relate to the world as if everyone is seeing it the same way we do.

Whether you realize it or not, we are communicating our deeply ingrained attitudes all the time. We may not verbalize them directly, but they are communicated in a myriad of ways—in our speaking, our actions, our choices, our likes and dislikes, our judgments, and our opinions.

The first step to having successful communication with others is to identify underlying attitudes and beliefs and begin to question them. Most importantly, it is essential to own your attitude and beliefs as *only one way to see the world*. It is one perspective. It is not the right one, or the best one. It is just the one that you formed over time. And just because it makes perfect sense to you doesn't make it right or mean that it will make sense to anyone else.

The next step is to accept others' perspectives as justifiable interpretations of the world they see. From their perspective, they cannot in this moment see it any other way. Arguing with their perspective will prevent effective communication because you are essentially telling them that their worldview is wrong, causing them to dig their heels in and argue even harder. Rather than arguing with their perspective, ask questions to help you understand their point of view. Look for commonalities and places where you can agree. The more open you are to understanding their point of view, the more open they will be to yours.

For effective communication to occur, it is necessary to adopt the attitude that both your perspective and their perspective are legitimate. This will enable authentic, meaningful communication to occur.

Insight: _____

_____

_____

_____

_____

_____

_____

What this means to me is: _____

_____

_____

_____

_____

_____

Ideas for Action

The boldest action I could take regarding this insight is: _____

_____

_____

_____

_____

_____

The action I am committing to is: _____

_____

_____

_____

_____

_____

Conscious Listening

Listening is arguably the most important part of communication, and yet we barely think about it. Most of us are unconscious of how we listen. We take listening for granted. How you listen shapes and influences absolutely everything you encounter.

I want you to think about a person who works with you or whom you oversee. Think of a one- to three-word description of that person. Your description is how you listen to him or her. It is an assessment based on *your* interpretation of the facts. Every time you interact with this person, this assessment filters your experience of him or her and influences what you hear, what you say, and even what the other person will say to you. It doesn't matter if your assessment is positive or negative; it shapes and influences the communication.

For example, let's say you have an employee, Joe, and your assessment is that he's lazy. Now imagine you are meeting with your staff, including Joe, to assign work that is critical to your company's success. How does your assessment of Joe affect how you'll listen to Joe and what you expect of Joe? What if Joe mentions a potential roadblock? How likely are you to take Joe's comment seriously rather than dismiss it as an attempt by Lazy Joe to get out of work? Now imagine that you think Joe is a hardworking team player. How does that impact how you'll respond to his suggestion?

The key is to become aware of how you listen to others and how your assessments made over time impact how you listen and act toward them, and, in response, how they listen and act toward you. Have you ever been with someone who thinks you are awesome? How does that influence how you act? Doesn't it make you feel empowered just to be around him or her? Now imagine being with someone who, despite your best efforts, has a low opinion of you. How do you act around him or her? Careful? Guarded? Now, think about a time when you have spoken to someone who is a know-it-all. What is that like for you? Was that person listening to you? How did his or her knowing it all impact your speaking? Was it comfortable or uncomfortable?

When you listen unconsciously, allowing your opinions to go unquestioned, you are being a know-it-all. You already "know-it-all" about the person you're talking with, and the result is you aren't really listening. You already know what he or she is going to say and how he or she is going to act. People are uncomfortable trying to talk to a know-it-all and usually give up. You have to ask yourself, is that how you want people to feel around you?

In order to bring out the best in your employees, you must choose to listen consciously. Conscious listening is about controlling your inner dialogue and truly being present to the other person. People act in accordance with the listening they are provided. We are unaware of the restrictive boxes we create for people to live inside of just by how we listen to them. Conscious listening allows for a whole new level of conversation to emerge. People become enlivened, and their natural creativity and enthusiasm are unleashed.

Insight: _____

_____

_____

_____

_____

_____

What this means to me is: _____

_____

_____

_____

_____

_____

Ideas for Action

The boldest action I could take regarding this insight is: _____

_____

_____

_____

_____

_____

The action I am committing to is: _____

_____

_____

_____

_____

_____

Your Narrator

I would like to introduce you to your narrator. "What narrator?" you might be thinking. That's your narrator. Your narrator is the voice in your head that has been chirping away for as long as you can remember. It's always there. It never turns off, and, most importantly, it's narrating what's happening before your eyes. "She's angry." "Why is he looking at me this way?" "My gosh, they always get this wrong." "This day is so great." "I think he's going to do well here."

Let's face it. You don't always have control over the things that are happening out there in life. The one thing you have total control over, though, is your narrator. You have total control over your thoughts. Getting a grip on your narrator is not about denying the things that are happening in your life. It's not about looking the other way in life and just thinking positive thoughts. No, it means you being responsible for your part in what's happening. Your narrator sets the expectations that people either are or aren't living up to. Your narrator is constantly judging and evaluating how life should look and often beating you and others up for not meeting those standards. Your narrator is commenting on what it sees rather passively, not caring about the wealth of information that it hasn't seen and is weeding out. Your narrator doesn't care about the whole story. It only cares about *its story*.

And so, in any interaction with another, you must begin to be aware that there are actually four people participating in the conversation. There's you. There's the other person. There's your narrator. And there's the other person's narrator. People often don't actually hear what you say. They hear what their narrator tells them you said. Getting a grip on your narrator doesn't mean you should stop being authentic with people about how you see things. It just means appreciating the fact that it's just how *you* see things, and it's not necessarily the way things actually are. Life would come to a grinding halt if we had to monitor every thought and research whether we had 100 percent of the data on any given subject. Understanding your narrator simply means understanding that *you are not your narrator*. You can think something else other than what your narrator is telling you.

Insight: _____
_____
_____
_____
_____
_____
_____

What this means to me is: _____
_____
_____
_____
_____
_____

Ideas for Action

The boldest action I could take regarding this insight is: _____
_____
_____
_____
_____
_____

The action I am committing to is: _____
_____
_____
_____
_____
_____

Be Willing to Learn

There is an underlying belief in the traditional model of supervision. It is that the supervisor knows best, needs to know all the answers, and must make all the decisions. This stems from the practice of early supervisors being placed on a raised platform so they could oversee their employees. This was believed to be necessary because the workforce was uneducated and inexperienced. Supervisors were seen as critical to the work getting done and therefore were responsible for directing everything and making all the decisions—and so they were expected to have all the answers.

Despite the fact that we have arguably the most educated workforce of all time, this belief prevails and continues to influence the actions of most supervisors and managers. This belief has outlived its usefulness and, in fact, limits what's possible. This belief stymies communication because you are unconsciously ruling out ideas that contradict your own. You may shoot down ideas without fully exploring them, and this may prevent you from seeing all the options.

Shifting this belief to one of being willing to learn not only opens up communication, it clears the way for innovation. You will have new levels of creativity when ideas are explored freely and people are able to challenge their limiting beliefs. Being willing to learn from your employees takes practice, but it is a way to empower and engage your employees to reach new heights. When they feel you are authentically open to learn from them, they will feel valued and appreciated.

As a supervisor or manager, chances are the traditional model has influenced your thinking and your actions. To start operating from the new belief (being willing to learn), you first must acknowledge your "I know best" thinking to your team. Let them know you are taking a different approach as a way of developing yourself and them, too. If you do not acknowledge your past way of interacting, your employees may be skeptical when you ask them questions. After you tell on yourself, they will help to remind you of your commitment if you fall back into your former habits.

Also, take time to inquire into the difference between how a supervisor who knows best might communicate versus how a supervisor who is willing to learn would communicate. You will start to see that there is a big disparity.

You may be concerned about the time involved in coming from this new perspective. It may seem that it is faster to just tell people what to do. This may be true, but ask yourself, "What is it costing long-term in the productivity and effectiveness of my employees?" This doesn't mean that you can never offer an answer or direction to your employee, but when you invest the time in learning from your employees, that investment will pay back big in the long run with employees who are highly engaged in the work they do.

Insight: _____
_____
_____
_____
_____
_____
_____

What this means to me is: _____
_____
_____
_____
_____
_____
_____

Ideas for Action

The boldest action I could take regarding this insight is: _____
_____
_____
_____
_____
_____
_____

The action I am committing to is: _____
_____
_____
_____
_____
_____
_____

Transactional vs. Transformational Conversations

Think about conversations as being on a spectrum. On one end is a transactional conversation. A transactional conversation is directive, a one-sided, informational conversation. Basically, it is like a monologue delivered to an audience. The underlying intention is to get compliance and or to deliver information. At the other end of the spectrum is a transformational conversation. This type of conversation broadens awareness and shifts the perspective of those involved. Change occurs in a transformational conversation as shared understanding results. A transformational conversation leaves people engaged and owning the conversation.

It is not that one type of conversation is good and the other is bad, or that one is right and the other is wrong, or even that one is better than the other. They are just different. The intentions for each are different, the experience of each is different, and, perhaps most importantly, the outcomes for each are different. On any given day we may fall at various points on the spectrum. Typically, though, the primary mode of conversation in the workplace, especially between manager and employee, is transactional, because it is the one we are most comfortable with.

Transactional conversations are necessary and serve a purpose. The biggest communication mistake that managers make is that they have *only* transactional conversations. An overreliance on this type of conversation often leads to people being frustrated because they feel talked at (not with), left out, and disengaged. There needs to be a balance between transactional conversations and transformational conversations. You need to think about the outcome that you want to have and decide which type of conversation is appropriate. If you have to deliver a challenging communication or you want people to change their minds, adopt a new point of view, get on board with a new policy, or engage their creativity, then a transformational conversation is probably in order. Although most people have experienced a transformational conversation at some point, by and large, they are not sure how to create the conditions for a transformational conversation to occur.

Here are some guidelines for having a transformational conversation:

- Listen consciously (see page 7).
- Create a context; explain the rationale for the perspective.
- Engage in the conversation without trying to control the outcome.
- Let go of the idea that there is only "one right way."
- Listen as if the person you are talking to will say something brilliant at any moment.
- Be open to having your mind changed.
- Appreciate the other's point of view and thinking style.

- Give people space for their reaction (rather than reacting to it).
- Come to a shared understanding. Be sure to ask what people heard, and discuss any discrepancies.

Insight: _____

_____

_____

_____

_____

_____

_____

What this means to me is: _____

_____

_____

_____

_____

_____

Ideas for Action

The boldest action I could take regarding this insight is: _____

_____

_____

_____

_____

_____

The action I am committing to is: _____

_____

_____

_____

_____

_____

Successful Communication is 100 Percent Your Responsibility

Yes, you read that correctly. Successful communication *is* 100 percent your responsibility. This advice goes against the grain; it bucks old adages like "It takes two to tango." In reality, this declaration of responsibility is not *the* truth. It's just a point of view; it's a way to begin to relate to your communication. Now, you might see this as a huge burden, but actually it's very freeing.

Usually when things go wrong, we often hope that it will turn out to be someone else's fault. When the contract doesn't arrive on time or when one of our employees is not performing up to par, it's easy to want to blame the other. And certainly, this is not about relieving the other parties from their responsibility. Still, relating to communication like it's 100 percent your responsibility gives you full control of the levers. It creates an exciting challenge for you to grow yourself. Imagine beginning to relate to life as if the results around you are a function of how you communicate. Rather than life occurring out here as a problem, life is now a measure of your ability to communicate effectively. It's constantly giving you feedback in every realm of how you're doing. Employee not performing well? It's feedback on how well you are communicating. Your boss not empowering you to do the job the way it needs to get done? Again, feedback on your ability to communicate.

Taking on this perspective will force you to be creative. It will force you to think from different perspectives, including the person's to whom you are speaking. So, yes, act as if communication is 100 percent your responsibility, and experience how much more freedom you have to positively impact the people around you.

Acting as if bringing out the best in your employees is 100 percent your responsibility will challenge your thinking and call into question your assumptions, leaving you free to create whole new ways of interacting.

Insight: _____
_____
_____
_____
_____
_____
_____

What this means to me is: _____
_____
_____
_____
_____
_____

Ideas for Action

The boldest action I could take regarding this insight is: _____
_____
_____
_____
_____
_____

The action I am committing to is: _____
_____
_____
_____
_____
_____

FEAR = False Evidence Appearing Real

We all know we have fears, but we often don't think about how fear influences our communication. Fear of the outcome of a conversation, fear of being misunderstood, fear of how people will respond, fear of looking bad, dumb, silly, etc., fear of being taken advantage of, fear of making a mistake, fear of being disliked, are a few examples of fears that impact communication.

One common fear that managers have is the fear of not knowing the answer. For many this stems from the "imposter syndrome," which is a fear of being "found out." In other words, some version of "I'm an imposter because I am really not smart (good, savvy, etc.) enough and someone is going to find out." This fear often manifests in an authoritative, directive, autocratic style of management.

Another common fear that managers have is the fear of making a mistake. The behaviors that accompany this fear are reluctance to make a decision, taking tentative actions, or shifting responsibility and blame onto others when a mistake has been made.

The bottom line is that fear limits your ability to communicate effectively. The first step to overcoming the constraints fear places on your communication is to become aware of the fears that you have. Begin to identify what you are avoiding and ask yourself why, to reveal the fears that are constraining you. Then, inquire into how the fear affects your communication. How do you compensate for the fear? Where do you let the fear control your actions?

Once you become aware of the fears you have, it is time to get curious about them. We are so busy trying to manage fear or work around fear or avoid fear or face fear that it never occurs to us to question fear; to explore where it came from, and ask whether it's necessary and relevant.

To question your fear, you have to ask yourself, "Is what I am afraid of real?" Now if you are in a dark alley and hear footsteps behind you gaining quickly, it might not be the best time to ask this question. However, if you have fear that stops you from taking action, from having conversations, from being who you want to be, then it is time to ask, "Is what I am afraid of *real*?"

"Real" is what is happening (or what happened) without any meaning attached to it—just the facts, as Joe Friday used to say. When you can separate out the facts from the meaning you added, you can begin to deconstruct your fear and see when your fear reaction is based on false evidence.

Whenever you feel afraid, think of the acronym F.E.A.R. —False Evidence Appearing Real—then question your fear. When you can identify that your fear is based on *false evidence*, it will give you the power to move through it. It is not about getting rid of your fear. It is about owning it as your issue and then asking yourself if it supports what you are committed to.

Insight: _____
_____
_____
_____
_____
_____
_____

What this means to me is: _____
_____
_____
_____
_____
_____

Ideas for Action

The boldest action I could take regarding this insight is: _____
_____
_____
_____
_____
_____

The action I am committing to is: _____
_____
_____
_____
_____
_____

Trust

We live in a world that demands that people earn our trust and that we earn theirs. What if trust isn't something for people to earn? What if, instead, trust is something to be given? Yes, it's true that people disappoint us sometimes. They let us down; they don't perform as they promised. They lie. They cut corners. Still, with all this evidence around us to not trust people, life requires that you trust. You must trust that others will stop for the red light. The day you hire someone, you must trust that he or she will do his or her job. There is no way for you to know whether he or she will or won't let you down. The people who work for you must trust that you are not going to undermine them; otherwise they will be overly cautious and tentative, preventing them from effectively fulfilling their job function.

The problem with asking people to earn our trust is that it starts from a place of mistrust. What if the job of the people around you was not to earn your trust, but instead to exceed your every expectation? What if it was their job to go blow the doors off their creativity and find more and more ways to amaze you, more and more ways to take your breath away with their performance? If you want that type of performance around you, you're going to have to give trust freely, fully, and willingly. You're going to have to find ways to communicate that you've given your trust. When you give people your trust and they know it, it makes them stronger. It frees them to take their attention off of you and really go for it. When people know you trust them, it causes them to believe more in themselves. Forcing people to earn your trust creates co-dependency and doubt.

Frankly, having others earn your trust is rather silly—they are already working for you and so you've already given it to them. Holding it back serves no purpose. Now this doesn't mean that you don't want to challenge people with high expectations so that you can learn who they are and how best to direct their talents. But when you give the challenge, make sure they know you are behind them. Make sure they know you've given them your trust.

Insight: _____

_____

_____

_____

_____

_____

_____

What this means to me is: _____

_____

_____

_____

_____

_____

Ideas for Action

The boldest action I could take regarding this insight is: _____

_____

_____

_____

_____

_____

The action I am committing to is: _____

_____

_____

_____

_____

_____

Authenticity

What does it mean to be authentic in the world of business? Is there value in it? This question, of course, assumes, as many of us do, that the world of business isn't part of life, meaning that it doesn't involve human beings. Human beings crave authenticity. In other areas of life, we do appreciate the opportunity to be fully heard, and so there's no reason to think that authenticity doesn't have a legitimate place in the world of business.

Being authentic doesn't mean that you must sit around a boardroom telling people how much you love them, anymore than it means sitting around and telling them how awful they are. Being authentic simply means sharing how the world occurs *for you*, and doing so in such a way that it creates freedom.

As a supervisor and leader, there is great value to be had by creating a culture of authenticity. It allows people to move past the things that often cause organizations to stall. Your number one task as a leader is to find ways to have people perform powerfully, and nothing disempowers people more than gossip or upset or even just experiencing fear caused by a challenge that lies ahead. People need an outlet to express the negative conversations that weigh them down and stop them. Allow people to authentically share their concerns; this can prevent them from getting stuck in their negativity.

The fine line that a supervisor must walk is to not let it turn into a gripe session. You must develop the ability to hear what people have to say and not do anything with it; don't argue with it or agree with it, just *get it,* so they are freed up to perform. Then remind them of their commitment.

A culture of authenticity carries with it the responsibility of every member to the long-term health and prosperity of the organization, as well as a commitment to shed anything that gets in the way. Being authentic doesn't mean that someone gets to verbally vomit on you and then you have to clean up the mess. It means creating a space for yourself and others to say what's true for them in that moment so you can be free to powerfully move on to what's next.

Insight: _____
_____
_____
_____
_____
_____
_____

What this means to me is: _____
_____
_____
_____
_____
_____

Ideas for Action

The boldest action I could take regarding this insight is: _____
_____
_____
_____
_____
_____

The action I am committing to is: _____
_____
_____
_____
_____
_____

What World Are You Describing?

Have you ever noticed that we spend a lot of our time speaking about what already happened? The world that's happening before your eyes is a result; meaning that it's happening and it's a result of what already happened. In that sense, there isn't anything you can do about it. You can't do anything about the house that's already built or where the market closed today. Most of us are not aware that when we are speaking about what's happening or even what's happened, there is another world that presents itself in thought—the world of the future, the world of our standards and ideals.

The world as it is occurring is always getting measured against your own personal standards and ideals. There's a way you want the world to be in concept, and then there's a way that you perceive what's actually happened. So we go into a quarterly meeting and someone reports out on the financial situation of the company based on last quarter's results. We didn't hit our mark, and you notice that a knot starts to form in your stomach. And then someone demands an explanation for the results, and we spend our time trying to come up with a good explanation for our failure. Imagine what would happen if someone in the room carefully raised his or her hand and said, "But sir, it's done. It's the past. There's nothing we can do about it now."

A lot of our time is spent focused upon that which we've already created because we think it gives us access to something. In truth, it does have some value. We certainly can learn something from our past, but really it's that world that lies in the background, the one filled with our hopes for the future, that we really care about. And so the point here is for you to be aware of which world you are speaking about—the past or the future. Are you consumed with what's already done? Or are you consumed with where you want to go?

Imagine if, rather than starting his speech with "I have a dream...," Martin Luther King Jr. began his speech with "I have a couple of things I'd like to point out that I don't like..." Your job as a leader is to capture people's imagination—to focus them on what's possible. Your job is to get them thinking. Yes, the past can teach us some things, but keep in mind that the knowledge of the past is only worthwhile to the extent that you have your focus on what you want to create. What's happening before your eyes is done, and there's nothing you can do about it. Let it go, and start describing the world you *want* to see. Ask questions of others about how we can build it. People are moved forward by describing to them where you want to go, not where you've been, and so make sure you're clear what world you are describing.

Insight: _____

_____

_____

_____

_____

_____

_____

What this means to me is: _____

_____

_____

_____

_____

_____

Ideas for Action

The boldest action I could take regarding this insight is: _____

_____

_____

_____

_____

_____

The action I am committing to is: _____

_____

_____

_____

_____

_____

Be Clear

You probably think this passage is about speaking with clarity and precision. On some level, that's true. Really, though, the point is to remind you that as well as being a supervisor and a leader, you are a human being. Although this is obvious, you know that sometimes you forget this. You forget that you get upset because good supervisors aren't supposed to. You forget that your mind gets cluttered with all the many things there are for you to do. You didn't get the job of leader by being ineffective or not being able to make room for a lot of things on your plate. Still, you must realize that holding all of those things in your head and dealing with all of your internal processing has an impact on you. When you are not clear in your mind and your body, you are not clear in your communication.

It is easy in the hustle and bustle of our daily lives for us to minimize the importance of taking the time to get ourselves clear. It often seems that the most important thing is to keep moving on to the next thing. It isn't.

How many times have you been short with someone because all the things rumbling around in your head distracted you? How many times have plans gotten confused because you didn't take care of the upset that was caused by a meeting you had with your boss two hours prior to delegating the task?

It's your job to be clear, and so you must find ways to get yourself clear, to remove all the clutter that is floating around in your mind, so that you can deliver powerful and effective communication. Whether you make a list of all the thoughts in your head, or meditate, or share your "clutter" with a trusted colleague or coach, or find some other method for gaining clarity, commit to taking the time and devoting the energy to being clear, because it is essential for effective communication to occur. Just remember, if you aren't clear (in every sense of the phrase), your communication won't be either.

Insight: _____

_____

_____

_____

_____

_____

_____

What this means to me is: _____

_____

_____

_____

_____

_____

Ideas for Action

The boldest action I could take regarding this insight is: _____

_____

_____

_____

_____

_____

The action I am committing to is: _____

_____

_____

_____

_____

_____

Language is Creative

Walk through any museum, see the great works of art, and appreciate the labor of a painting or a sculpture. Go to the symphony and hear the beauty of the music as it seems to flow effortlessly from the musicians' instruments. Read the financial news and find a glowing article about the company that an astute businesswoman has built. These are all great acts of innovation, creativity, and beauty. Still, the lesson to be learned is that before these were amazing acts, they were mere thoughts in someone's head. Thought—language—is the first step in the creative process. This is always the case. Nothing exists in reality that was created by a human being that didn't live once as thought.

If you are the head of a high-performing team, what you see today is a result of what you thought in the past. If you are the head of a not-so-high-performing team, it resulted from the same. Either is a result in some way, shape, or form of what you thought. It's not that you had the exact thought, "I'm going to create a subpar team." However, if you trace your thinking back, you will find a link between your thinking and the results that are showing up.

An excellent place to look is at the conversations you've been having with your team members. What has been the content of those conversations? Have you talked most about how hard it's going to be to survive in the bad economy? Or how difficult it is to motivate people? Or how challenged you are by their performance? Or have you been talking about how proud you are of their growth? Or how amazed you are at what they've achieved despite the odds? This doesn't mean you have to live in denial and not discuss frankly the results that people have produced. Just be clear when you speak about those results that you're speaking about results and you're doing so to get grounded in what the team has produced, not in what your team is capable of producing. Begin to see the connection between what you say and what shows up, including and especially people's actions. Experiment and learn to leverage the awesome creative power there is in language.

Insight: _____
_____
_____
_____
_____
_____
_____

What this means to me is: _____
_____
_____
_____
_____
_____
_____

Ideas for Action

The boldest action I could take regarding this insight is: _____
_____
_____
_____
_____
_____
_____

The action I am committing to is: _____
_____
_____
_____
_____
_____
_____

Focus on What Works

There are always things that are working in your department and things that aren't. Most people spend the vast majority of time and energy focusing on what doesn't work and trying to fix it. Now this might elicit the response, "Of course I do, that's how to improve" or "How else am I going to develop my employees?"

Focusing on what doesn't work actually slows down growth and development. It can keep you stuck and prevent you from moving forward. The bottom line is that the way we have been trained to think about change has been wrong.

It is not that you should ignore what doesn't work, but be honest: how long have you been working on it? For most of us, it has been years of trying to improve the same thing, only to see incremental progress.

The first thing I want you to be clear about is this is not your fault. It's just a habitual way of thinking that we've all inherited. We learned to relate to others and ourselves as problems to be solved. We learned that life is a problem to be solved. Problem solving and focusing on what doesn't work drains us of energy. Seeing ourselves day after day, week after week, month after month, year after year, as endless problems to be solved is exhausting. No wonder people have the Monday morning blues. A whole new week of problems to solve—woo hoo! No wonder people get disengaged at work.

When you only focus on what doesn't work, it limits your thinking and your capacity to attain the results you really want.

What if there was another way to get what you want? Another way to achieve your goals? And what if it could be energizing, empowering, and, most importantly, more effective? What if you didn't always have to feel you were broken in need of repair?

Focusing on what works is another way to view life. Think about it: if you want to be rich, you would not study poor people. If you want to be thin, you would not study overweight people. Success is not found by studying failure and doing the opposite. Success has a texture and depth all its own.

The areas that are working about you and your department are not by accident or luck or because the moon and the sun lined up just right. They work for reasons. When you discover what the reasons are, you start to unleash the source of your power.

Our greatest potential for learning is in our areas of strength, not in our weakness. When you recognize and acknowledge what works about you, your employees, and your department, you will begin to see everything differently, which will spark innovative thinking and whole new possibilities for action. This is the environment that allows the best in your employees to emerge.

Insight: _____

_____

_____

_____

_____

_____

_____

What this means to me is: _____

_____

_____

_____

_____

_____

Ideas for Action

The boldest action I could take regarding this insight is: _____

_____

_____

_____

_____

_____

The action I am committing to is: _____

_____

_____

_____

_____

_____

Let People Be Where They Are

That's right, I said it. Let them be. You are a supervisor. You are not a counselor, a priest, a judge, or a jury. Your job as a supervisor is to set a course, establish a vision, and achieve it. The world of communication can sometimes get messy, especially at work. When this happens, let people be where they are. This doesn't mean ignore them. It doesn't mean tell them to just suck it up. It means to honor them as adults. They don't need you to fix things for them, and the more that you do, the more they'll rely on you to do so. It's not your job. Your job is to want more for them than they want for themselves. Your job is expecting them to be great. Your job is to be surprised by people.

And one of the best things about letting people be where they are is that you are allowed to be where you are. There is nothing more frustrating than to be excited about the possibilities you see for the future and have your excitement dashed because you have to deal with someone's complaint about the course of action that you've chosen. People get upset, and mostly it has nothing to do with you. Again this doesn't mean you should dismiss them. Dismissing people is not letting people be where they are. You move when you're ready, and so do others.

Letting people be where they are is simply letting them be where they are; not resisting where they are, adding meaning to where they are, or thinking they should be somewhere other than where they are. People have to move through their spaces. If you let people be where they are, they are less likely to get stuck, and then they can move to acceptance or even to championing the new idea. It is respectful to let people be where they are, because you are honoring their point of view as valid.

Finally, and perhaps most importantly, letting people be where they are doesn't mean you have to wait for them. No, no, no. You should move with the joy and passion that caused you to create your vision in the first place. Clearing the pathway with that type of energy is the best thing you can do for people when they are stuck. If you clear a bright pathway, they will follow. Or they won't, but at least you'll know where they stand.

Insight: _____
_____
_____
_____
_____
_____
_____

What this means to me is: _____
_____
_____
_____
_____
_____

Ideas for Action

The boldest action I could take regarding this insight is: _____
_____
_____
_____
_____
_____

The action I am committing to is: _____
_____
_____
_____
_____
_____

Welcome Dissent

As leaders, sometimes we don't want to hear the bad stuff. We don't want to hear the reasons why not. We don't want to hear what people are gossiping and complaining about. We don't want to hear it mostly because we don't know what to do with dissent. That's where the shift needs to occur, because the more you try to do something with the dissent, the more it will grow. Consider there is nothing to do with dissent except hear it. You're the leader. You don't need to fix every person's problem. That's not your job. Your job is to articulate, design, and set a course to achieve some vision. And, frankly, it's a bit crazy to expect that people won't have dissent to your vision.

The value in being open to the dissent of others is that the more you can give people the space to say what they need to say, the more they will move through any upset they have. People have a fundamental need to be heard. Usually they understand when a decision other than what they want is made, but what leaves them stuck is when they are not being heard.

The other benefit of welcoming dissent is that it allows you to clarify your message. Often you'll find that people haven't heard what you said; they've heard their own interpretation of what you said. That's why managers often resist dissent, because it is hard to accept that their motives and authority are being questioned. Managers can't imagine why their employees aren't as excited as they are at the possibility they envision. Managers often struggle to understand why their employees don't realize that the manager really and truly wants both the organization and the employees to thrive.

Here's the key: dissent is not personal. It really has nothing to do with you or even your idea. It's just people's way of dealing with a new idea or new way of doing things. The more you can welcome it without resistance, the more you can fine-tune what you've said so people understand where you are coming from, and the more you can help them see that perhaps what you're saying is not what they're hearing. The bottom line is, whether you open yourself up to dissent or not, it's there. People have it, and so your task as a leader is to move people forward powerfully into action—and one of the best ways to do that is to welcome dissent.

Insight: _____
_____
_____
_____
_____
_____
_____

What this means to me is: _____
_____
_____
_____
_____
_____
_____

Ideas for Action

The boldest action I could take regarding this insight is: _____
_____
_____
_____
_____
_____
_____

The action I am committing to is: _____
_____
_____
_____
_____
_____
_____

"Because" is a Four-Letter Word

Is knowing the cause of something really a bad thing? No, of course it isn't. Often, though, the word "because" is not followed with an explanation of why we were so successful in the latest project or why we are going to be successful next year and have our most profitable year ever. "Because" is typically followed with the reasons why the things we want to achieve are not possible. As a supervisor you often will need to hear the reasons why not or the pitfalls to your ideas. In those instances, "because" is being used as a substitute for four-letter words like "stop" or "don't" or "can't." "Stop this course of action." "Don't do it. You'll be sorry." "We just can't do this."

So what do you do when someone comes to you with his or her version of "because"? First, have compassion for it. The person is genuinely stuck and may have some legitimate points to make. However, the fact that someone has legitimate points to make doesn't mean that he or she is right; that what you are proposing can't be done. You must remember that your job as a leader and supervisor is to make things happen that the current reality says isn't possible. It's your job to move the ball forward even when there is a defense rushing you. So your job is to propose things that don't seem possible and then find a way to organize your people to make your goal possible.

So when you hear "because," that's a prompt for you to listen intently, thank the person, promise that you'll take what he or she said under advisement (and really do so), and then ask him or her something like, "If I decide to go ahead despite your recommendation, can I count on your support? I know that what I'm proposing is new and different, and it's going to take all the creativity we can get." When you don't get lost in "becauses," you don't fall victim to someone else's story; instead you are spinning a new tale.

Insight: _____

_____

_____

_____

_____

_____

_____

What this means to me is: _____

_____

_____

_____

_____

_____

Ideas for Action

The boldest action I could take regarding this insight is: _____

_____

_____

_____

_____

_____

The action I am committing to is: _____

_____

_____

_____

_____

_____

What You Want is What You Want...

And the barriers are the barriers. "What?" you may be thinking. Human beings have this amazing capacity to make associations. It's one of our most powerful abilities. On the other hand, we are not so great at breaking associations. In other words, we're not very adept at questioning our thinking critically and seeing where perhaps we've put things together that don't belong together. In fact, sometimes we put things together and don't realize that we've in fact put two different and distinct things together. I've found that this is the case with the two things "what you want" and "the barriers to what you want." Have you ever noticed that when people communicate about their goals, they spend what seems like a split second talking about what they want and then they instantly move into talking about the barriers to what they want?

Yes, there are barriers in life, and yes, sometimes it is necessary to talk about the barriers. However, the reality is that people don't really question this association. They don't question whether the barrier actually does have something to do with what they want. They don't question whether the way they see it—the way they see the path from A (where they are) to B (what they want) —really and truly is the only pathway there.

Moreover, have you ever noticed that generally people only talk about barriers that have them stopped? Really every action along the way from A to B is a barrier. In fact, if you look at all of the actions required to fulfill a goal, most of them are not perceived as a barrier at all. The point is that there is something available as a supervisor to get people's attention off the barrier and have them start talking about the goal – what they want. Our goals are never really linear pathways from A to B. They are rich worlds ripe for an individual's (or an organization's) growth and development.

Take the very basic business goal of making $1,000,000 in profit next year. To achieve that goal is going to involve building something. It's going to involve developing competencies in people. It will likely require building structures. When you have the person describe the depth of the world he or she wants to create, you are helping him or her to get unstuck from the things that, for whatever reason, he or she perceives as barriers. You are helping him or her to open his or her thinking to great possibilities.

"But what about the barrier?" you may be thinking. The bottom line is that in this moment, people cannot see a solution, and, in fact, they don't even really know whether the barrier is actually a barrier at all. In that moment, the only barrier to the project moving forward *is them*. They are stuck in their own thinking and they need *you* to have a conversation with them to remind them of their commitment and the world they want to create.

Insight: _____

_____

_____

_____

_____

_____

_____

What this means to me is: _____

_____

_____

_____

_____

_____

Ideas for Action

The boldest action I could take regarding this insight is: _____

_____

_____

_____

_____

_____

The action I am committing to is: _____

_____

_____

_____

_____

_____

The Whole Story

As a supervisor, your job, as you know, is to lead people. One of the most effective ways to lead them is to tell them where you're going. Tell them the whole story. Tell them where you're going. Tell them why you've decided to go there. Tell them what you are expecting from them. Tell them what you know and what you don't know about where you're going. Tell them everything you can. Don't misunderstand, you're not telling them so they can vote on where you want to take them. You're telling them to paint a picture of the future. You're telling the whole story because if you don't, their minds are going to go berserk filling in the gaps. When people experience gaps in their future, they can lose faith. And yes, of course, there are going to be gaps, so you want to tell them that, too. You want to tell them that you're counting on them to close the gaps in the picture and that today, they might not know how. Tell them you don't know how!

People absolutely need a strong leader but they also need to know where they are going. When they know where they are going, they can see themselves in the future. They can begin to create it for themselves. They can ask questions about it. Heck, they might even start to get excited about it.

It's not necessary to have this type of conversation every day, every week, or even every month. But periodically, if you sit down with your people and just share, it will not only create freedom for them, it will create freedom for you. By the nature of your position, you've been given the authority to some degree to set the course. Your authority alone doesn't necessarily give you the freedom to ask people to follow you. Telling them where you're going, telling the whole story, will give you the freedom to lead.

Insight: _____
_____
_____
_____
_____
_____
_____

What this means to me is: _____
_____
_____
_____
_____
_____

Ideas for Action

The boldest action I could take regarding this insight is: _____
_____
_____
_____
_____
_____

The action I am committing to is: _____
_____
_____
_____
_____
_____

Don't Should on Yourself!

Everywhere you turn, someone is trying to give you advice. Heck, I wrote this book to give you advice. In our culture, we've come to trust experts more than ourselves. Now, on some level, there are good and legitimate reasons for that. A surgeon dedicated her life to knowing how to operate on you. I've dedicated my life to understanding the nuances of communication and bringing out the best in people. You've dedicated yourself to whatever field you are in. At the same time, you need to find what works for you in all realms—especially in the area of communication.

When you "should" on yourself, you are making yourself wrong for not doing something or being something. When you do that, you are missing the things that you do. When you do it to others, you're missing the great things that they do. It is not that the word "should" is taboo and is never to be spoken at work. I'm talking about the times when we beat others or ourselves up for things we feel we *should* be doing, but we are not. Have you ever noticed that very often when you do that, it makes no difference? All it does is make you feel bad about yourself and others.

When you catch yourself "shoulding" on yourself or another, you are no longer at the helm of the ship. Captain Fear has taken over and your mind is on autopilot, doing nothing but damage. In that moment, stop. Stop and ask yourself one very simple question: "I appreciate what I should do, but what am I actually willing to do to move forward? What's the next step I am willing to commit to?" Sit quietly and wait for an answer. As a leader, as a human being, all you can do is the next thing you actually know and are willing to do. Despite the claims of multi-taskers, you really cannot do more than one thing at a time—not consciously anyway. In any moment, you are doing one thing. What's the *next* thing for you to do? Perhaps it's just to stop "shoulding" on yourself so you have the freedom to lead.

Insight: _____

_____

_____

_____

_____

_____

_____

What this means to me is: _____

_____

_____

_____

_____

_____

Ideas for Action

The boldest action I could take regarding this insight is: _____

_____

_____

_____

_____

_____

The action I am committing to is: _____

_____

_____

_____

_____

_____

What Are You Building?

What are you building? Do you know? How long has it been since you've sat down and asked yourself that question? How can you lead if you don't know what you're building? Yes, yes, I know, you're busy. The demands on you and your time seem endless. But have you stopped to consider that those demands are *the result of what you've built?* In any given moment in time, we are experiencing the results of the world that we've built. Even though it seems like it, the world you're experiencing didn't just happen by accident. You didn't create all of it. Sure, some of it you inherited. Guess what? Today, it's still yours. The good employees are yours. The bad ones are yours. They are all your result.

The choice I want to lay before you is this—you can either continue to deal with the negative unintended consequences of what you've built *or* you can build what you really want. Choose. If you are suffering from not enough time, then your task is to build a world where you have enough time. If your employees are not engaged in their work, then it's your task to build a work unit where people are engaged in their work. The most basic question you can ask yourself is whether you've built the best operating unit possible. Your work group (or department) is a thing. Have you built it to work?

What does this have to do with communication? Simple: all of the communication "issues" that you experience today are a result of what you've built. One way to be an effective communicator is to build a better "ship" that's designed to give you what you want. Do you need to deal with the demands of today? Of course you do. The real question is, "How many more tomorrows do you want to keep dealing with the same demands and the same issues in communication?"

Insight: _____
_____
_____
_____
_____
_____
_____

What this means to me is: _____
_____
_____
_____
_____
_____

Ideas for Action

The boldest action I could take regarding this insight is: _____
_____
_____
_____
_____
_____

The action I am committing to is: _____
_____
_____
_____
_____
_____

Imagine It from Scratch

Can you really build something from scratch? Is that really what's required to be successful? Scrap the whole thing and start over? Of course not. What you must understand is this: your business, your organization, your work group is a thing; it's a system. Your task as a leader is to build the very best operating "thing" that you can. Sound impersonal? Perhaps. But perhaps the reason that our organizations suffer from so much organizational drag caused by lack of engagement of their employees is because we don't build our organizations to be what they are. The people in organizations are not bound by blood or friendship. They are bound by purpose, and that purpose is the organization's purpose.

The problem for most supervisors is they try to walk the line of keeping people happy while feeling an internal (and sometimes external) pressure to produce results. And so you sit there at your desk and try to envision the direction the organization should move in. You begin to craft a vision of the future, and just as you begin to get excited, the conflict rears its ugly head. "Joe will never go for that. He doesn't like participating in that way." "We can't do that. The computer system has already been built to accomplish it this other way." Your high standards of excellence are demanding something of you, your heart is demanding something of you, but you find yourself compromising what you know you want to do. And you've done this not because you're weak, you've done it simply because you commingled your vision of the future with your picture of the past. You haven't maintained a clear separation between what you've already created and what you want to create.

In the end, you won't build your organization from scratch. It's not necessary that you do, but you must *imagine it from scratch*. You must see that there's the work group you have and the work group you want to create. There are two things! Don't confuse them. Your mind craves clarity. It thrives on clarity even if you don't know how to get it today. Even if there are certain things it's going to take a while to actually put in place. Even if some of those things can never really be actualized. You must resolve the negative tension for your mind by clearly articulating where you want to go independent from where you are. When you do this, you create positive tension for your mind—creative tension. You can stop walking the tightrope of pleasing people and start building your future. You'll be free to build your future. You'll be free to communicate powerfully what you really want and ask people to join you in creating it.

Insight: _____

_____

_____

_____

_____

_____

_____

What this means to me is: _____

_____

_____

_____

_____

_____

_____

Ideas for Action

The boldest action I could take regarding this insight is: _____

_____

_____

_____

_____

_____

_____

The action I am committing to is: _____

_____

_____

_____

_____

_____

_____

Their Feelings are Their Business

Seriously, how your employees feel is their business. This doesn't give you license to ignore or squash the expression of the feelings of others. The point is, it is not your job to fix or change their feelings or thoughts. Each of us has been bestowed with this very wonderful thing—it's called choice. People are working with you and for you because they choose to. No one is holding a gun to their head. Again, this does not give you free rein to make people's lives miserable. Chances are you are committed to exactly the opposite because you picked up and are reading this book. Still, you have enough trouble managing your own emotional world without managing another's. Taking care of yourself and your emotions—i.e., your business—is the very best thing you can do for people. You'll be surprised at how much freedom you have to let people communicate what they need to communicate. You'll be surprised at how much better a listener you will become naturally, because—well, frankly, you'll find that you are actually listening rather than worrying about how you're going to deal with the communication.

People are resourceful. Yes, they need to be listened to. Yes, they need to express themselves. Those are all things that you can do for them. But you cannot fix their emotions. Their emotions are their business, so keep your nose clear of them.

Here are some suggested dos and don'ts:

Do	Don't
• Listen without judgment	• Say, I know how you feel
• Give your full attention	• Say, You shouldn't feel that way
• Provide parameters (i.e., no name calling, gossip, etc.)	• Say, I'll take care of it
• Say it sounds like you are upset (angry, frustrated, disappointed, etc.) so they know you heard them	• React to their reaction
	• Judge their reaction
	• Multitask while they are talking
• Say, what actions can you take to help improve this situation?	• Criticize them for coming to you
• Acknowledge them for coming to you and not gossiping, letting it fester, etc.	• Gossip about them for talking to you

Insight: _____
_____
_____
_____
_____
_____
_____

What this means to me is: _____
_____
_____
_____
_____
_____

Ideas for Action

The boldest action I could take regarding this insight is: _____
_____
_____
_____
_____
_____

The action I am committing to is: _____
_____
_____
_____
_____
_____

Your Pillars of Communication

Quite often, I find that supervisors are not powerful communicators because they haven't identified their pillars of communication. Put quite simply, your pillars of communication answer the question, "What do you stand for?" In other words, what is the thing or things that you most want to be expressed in the world? Are your pillars excellence, creativity, and inspiration? Are they integrity, compassion, and wealth? Or are they practicality, dignity, and respect? You may have more than two or three pillars—things that are important to you—but I've found that people cannot focus on more than two or three at a time, and any one pillar is often the type of thing you can spend a lifetime mastering.

What does this have to do with communication? Each one of us communicates based on how we see the world, and if your internal world —your thinking—is not clearly defined for you, the result is that the outside world tends to push and pull you in all sorts of different directions. Lack of clarity in your mind and in what you stand for leads you to give mixed signals to people. One day you are asking them to be more creative in their work, and the next day you are asking them to move faster because your boss is hounding you for an answer. You can find yourself drifting back and forth like the wind simply because you are not clear what it is that makes up the foundation not just of who you are and how you operate, but of what you want to create in the world. Certainly, speed and creativity are not inherently at odds with one another. The point is, if push comes to shove, which one are you going to stand for? If "creativity" wins for you over "efficiency and speed," then the most appropriate action in the scenario described above might be to go speak with your boss rather than your employees about the issue at hand. And, yes, sometimes, despite your commitment, your bosses' pillar for efficiency will win out, but don't let that stop you. What do you want to create long term? How do you want them to relate to you in the long run, because guess what? If they demand speed and you give them speed at the expense of creativity and never bring your pillar of creativity into their awareness, your voice is going to get squashed. You are very quickly going to become someone you are not, your communication will suffer, and your employees will be unable to bring their best.

Insight: _____

_____

_____

_____

_____

_____

_____

What this means to me is: _____

_____

_____

_____

_____

_____

Ideas for Action

The boldest action I could take regarding this insight is: _____

_____

_____

_____

_____

_____

The action I am committing to is: _____

_____

_____

_____

_____

_____

Speak as if...

Want to transform your communication, speak as if.... Speak as if the people around you are as smart or smarter than you are, even if they're not. Speak as if the people around you are inspired to do their best, even if it doesn't feel like they are. Speak as if people want to be challenged, even if you have tons of evidence that suggests they don't. This *is* about denial. Yes, let me say that again. If that's what it takes to transform your communication, then this *is* about denial. No one wants to be spoken to as if he or she is "less than" and as if he or she doesn't care (even if he or she doesn't). Why? Because people care, and they want to care. They like to care. It's your job as a leader to show them that it's okay to care. It's okay to be enlivened by their work. It's okay to want to give their best. It's okay to want to be challenged. It's really fine. It's all right. Those things are good things, and it's okay to feel them, to be them, and to want them.

We've all been "raised" in a world that tells us it's not okay to want these things, talk about these things, care about these things. That it's especially not okay to declare, "I'm excited to go to work," and yet we want to be excited and engaged. We all want to feel alive.

So you want to transform your communication and your ability to bring out the best in people, give up your preconceived notions about your team and speak as if....

Insight: _____

_____

_____

_____

_____

_____

_____

What this means to me is: _____

_____

_____

_____

_____

_____

Ideas for Action

The boldest action I could take regarding this insight is: _____

_____

_____

_____

_____

_____

The action I am committing to is: _____

_____

_____

_____

_____

_____

Limiting Beliefs about Communication

A very valuable exercise is to log all of your limiting beliefs about communication. Any belief you have that is not examined consciously has control over you. Despite the fact that you're not thinking about it consciously, it can still creep in and frame your interactions with people. When you take the time to list them and think about whether your belief actually serves you, then you can really choose it. It's absolutely fine to examine a belief and decide that you do, in fact, believe it. At least you'll know that when you experience the consequences (good or bad) of that belief, you are at the source of it.

You might actually find that just the very act of listing them and bringing them into your awareness is all that is needed to begin to cause a transformation in your ability to communicate effectively with people. In fact, you might find yourself thinking, "No wonder it always turns out this way with _____" or "Makes sense now why I never get _____." Just the simple act of examining your beliefs can transform how you communicate.

So take some time and make a list. Here are some questions to help you identify your limiting beliefs:

- What do you expect from people in communication?
- What are you listening for?
- How does your opinion or judgment about the person you are talking to impact your communication?
- What do you think is the "right" way to communicate? Where did you learn that?
- What are the "shoulds" you believe about communication?

Once you have identified these beliefs, begin to notice how they influence your communication. Then notice if the results these beliefs are producing are results you want. If not, start to adopt new beliefs about communication. Ask yourself, how might I think differently about communication to achieve a different result? You will be amazed at how powerful the act of questioning your beliefs is and the new possibilities for communication it opens up for you.

Insight: _____

_____

_____

_____

_____

_____

_____

What this means to me is: _____

_____

_____

_____

_____

_____

Ideas for Action

The boldest action I could take regarding this insight is: _____

_____

_____

_____

_____

_____

The action I am committing to is: _____

_____

_____

_____

_____

_____

A Better Outcome than You Imagined

Have you ever noticed that you pretty much get just about what you expect in life? This applies as well to our communication. Just look; think about how you communicate with people. Are you open to being surprised by them? Are you open to someone responding other than how you expected him or her to respond? Begin today: before any significant conversation, imagine a better outcome than you typically would have imagined.

This isn't magic. Think about it this way. Suppose you have someone who, over time, you've come to believe is stubborn. Imagine you call him into the office for what you feel is going to be a difficult conversation. You say what you need to say, and then there's dead silence on his part. He is just looking off into space, maybe shaking his head. "Uh oh," your mind says, "here he goes again. His old stubborn ways." So you jump into the silence and say something reactive, trying to fix his stubbornness. Now he's been provoked and he digs in. "See that," you say to yourself, "I knew it." You're so smart...such a savvy communicator. What if it turns out that in that silence, he was just thinking? All he was doing was sorting out what you said, just trying to get his mind around it and understand it. In fact, he was just about to ask a question when you jumped in with what seemed like an attack.

This type of result is typical because, as communicators, we primarily spend our time thinking about how to communicate to the person who *we think* we're about to communicate to, rather than imagining any other possibility. People are not a list of attributes. They are not made to be put in the boxes that you've put them in, and ultimately the cost of doing so is not only to them; it's to you. When you put someone in a box and relate to him or her as such, you've done the same to yourself. You decided, "Joe is _____ so I must act this way to counteract it." Sure, people tend toward certain behaviors. Yes, people have personalities, but people also share one other thing in common: they want to grow. They want to experience life beyond the bounds of how the world relates to them and how they relate to themselves. Give them the space to experience that growth. Imagine a better outcome and communicate from there.

Insight: _____

_____

_____

_____

_____

_____

_____

What this means to me is: _____

_____

_____

_____

_____

_____

_____

Ideas for Action

The boldest action I could take regarding this insight is: _____

_____

_____

_____

_____

_____

_____

The action I am committing to is: _____

_____

_____

_____

_____

_____

_____

Ask for What You Want

In order to ask for what you want, first you have to know what it is you want. Most of the time we have learned to settle for what we think we can have. We don't ask for what we really want because we try to avoid the disappointment of being turned down or rejected or made to feel foolish. Better to be the cause of our own disappointment by deciding not to even ask.

To have empowered and engaged employees who produce results, you have to be empowered and engaged. You cannot be empowered and engaged if you have given up on what you want. You have to get clear that you are entitled to want what you want.

Once you know what you want, then you can begin to identify who can help you achieve it. Truly successful people know that asking for help is necessary to attaining any goal. Lone rangers are a myth. It is virtually impossible to achieve any result on your own. There is always someone who contributed to the result being produced.

The challenge many people have with asking is that they assume the answer is going to be no, so they are tentative in making the request or they attempt to manipulate the person into saying yes. Then it doesn't feel like they are being asked so much as told. To overcome this, ask yourself: What is the assessment you have about a negative response to your request? Where did you get that belief? Are you willing to let that assessment go to have what you want?

If you are asking someone to do something or to help you with something, he or she must have the freedom to say no; otherwise, you are not really asking. You are *telling* but pretending to be asking. If no is not an option—i.e., you need an employee to complete something—then direct him or her to do the thing and ask what support he or she needs to complete it.

Another difficulty with asking is the tendency to not want to impose on anyone. The assumption here is people don't want to say yes or that people don't want to help if they can. We add a lot of complexity to the simple act of asking for something! Most people love having the opportunity to say yes to helping or contributing to someone's success. Don't you love it when you can help someone? When you know you made a difference in someone's life? Doesn't it feel awesome? Why would you want to rob someone of that feeling?

Asking does require a readiness to trust. Trust that the person is capable of deciding to say yes or no to our request. Trust that the person will fulfill the request they have agreed to. Percy Ross, philanthropist and entrepreneur, said, "You've got to ask. Asking is, in my opinion, the world's most powerful and neglected secret to success and happiness." The game is being willing to ask for what you want!

Insight: _____

_____

_____

_____

_____

_____

_____

What this means to me is: _____

_____

_____

_____

_____

_____

Ideas for Action

The boldest action I could take regarding this insight is: _____

_____

_____

_____

_____

_____

The action I am committing to is: _____

_____

_____

_____

_____

_____

Power Over vs. Power With

Think about the way you communicate with your employees. Is the context of your communication something like, "I am the boss, do as I tell you"? If so, that is the classic "power over" model of management. The main purpose is to get things done, not necessarily in the best way. This model treats employees as parts in a machine, a means to an end. It reduces people to their function within the organization, discounting their abilities to think, create, and innovate. In this model, the role of the supervisor is to watch over people to make sure they get their job done, much like a babysitter.

The focus of this communication is mostly reactionary, putting out fires, fixing what's perceived as broken. It's an orderly way of producing results, no fuss, no muss. But the disadvantages are many. People don't like to be treated like machines. They become disengaged, disgruntled, resigned. Eventually, they can become dependent on the supervisor for answers.

An alternative way of communicating is to use "power with," a shared power model. It creates a level playing field. Employees are involved in decision making and are more self-directed. Communication centers on creating a desired outcome. Learning is an integral part of the process. The staff is trusted to use their skills and abilities to produce results. The supervisor's role is to serve as a support and guide for learning and creating together.

The advantages of the "power with" model are many. It leads to engaged and empowered employees who enthusiastically participate in achieving the goals of the organization. New innovative solutions are developed and implemented, creating an edge over your competition. Gossip and cliques cease to exist because they are not necessary in a shared power model. The "power with" model can feel messy because creating is messy. It takes a willingness to trust, a deep respect for your people, and patience to fully embrace the "power with" paradigm.

Think of these two models as opposite ends of a spectrum. You are probably somewhere in between, sometimes sharing power, sometimes not. Most supervisors tend toward the "power over" end since it's more familiar. This in-between approach is confusing for your employees. Likely there are no clear parameters as to when you are sharing power and when you are not.

The "power over" model gives a sense of control. It feels less risky to be in charge and oversee everything. This is an illusion. This model fosters anger, frustration, disrespect, and resignation. These powerful emotions get played out somewhere, perhaps as gossiping, undermining behaviors, or sabotage. Each time you deal with one of these issues ignoring the underlying source (the "power over" model), you perpetuate the negative behaviors.

Begin today to develop your ability to share power. Look for places where you can give away control. As a first step, elicit suggestions from your employees. Where do they see improvements should be made? Implement those suggestions wherever possible. Acknowledge and appreciate all suggestions. If you truly want to empower and engage your employees and drive results and performance, then your job is to develop mastery in the "power with" model.

Insight: _____

_____

_____

_____

_____

_____

_____

What this means to me is: _____

_____

_____

_____

_____

_____

Ideas for Action

The boldest action I could take regarding this insight is: _____

_____

_____

_____

_____

_____

_____

The action I am committing to is: _____

_____

_____

_____

_____

_____

_____

The Opportunity of Challenging Communications

Most people do not like confrontations, nor do they look forward to challenging communications. There is a pervasive belief that these types of communications are unpleasant and difficult. In reality, a challenging communication is an extraordinary opportunity to develop your communication ability.

I once had a manager who used to always say, "It is easy to be great when things are great. Who are you going to be when things aren't great?" This is especially true for communication. It is relatively easy to communicate when things are great. When things are not great, when it is dicey, that's when real talent is required.

Imagine seeing challenging communications as a training ground for yourself. Think about how you might approach them differently if you knew you were going to make mistakes, because that is what you do when you are in training. Imagine the relief of going into the conversation not with it all figured out, but with a commitment to an outcome and discovering the best way to get there.

Embracing challenging conversations for the opportunity they provide is a much more empowering place to come from than being intimidated or frightened by them. In my experience, communicating from fear doesn't usually end up with happy, satisfied participants.

As a manager, you are going to have to engage in challenging, dicey, messy conversations at times. Sometimes you are going to get it all wrong and hate being a manager. Other times you are going to take into account that you are training yourself to master communication, and you will find your way through the muck and get to the other side having achieved the outcome you desired. That is going to be the conversation you remember and celebrate, because you moved yourself a little closer to mastery.

Insight: _____
_____
_____
_____
_____
_____
_____

What this means to me is: _____
_____
_____
_____
_____
_____

Ideas for Action

The boldest action I could take regarding this insight is: _____
_____
_____
_____
_____
_____

The action I am committing to is: _____
_____
_____
_____
_____
_____

Be the Change

It is so easy to look out and see all the things that are wrong at your organization or with your team. He should be more conscientious, she should stop complaining, they should work together better, etc. Seeing the gaps in performance and knowing what needs to be changed are part of a supervisor's role. In addition, being able to effect change is critical to your role as a successful manager.

The ultimate tool in your toolbox for effecting change is, as Gandhi said, "Be the change you wish to see in the world." This is not some esoteric concept. This has real-world, practical applications. You want people to work together better? You be more collaborative. You want him to be more conscientious? You be that way. You want complaining to end? Stop complaining and be solution oriented.

As the manager or supervisor, you are the leader of your team. They go where you lead whether you want to believe it or not. Who you are being impacts their behavior. Your ways of being have more influence over people's behavior than any other form of communication you convey. Being trumps everything. Here is an example: when you notice your significant other being withdrawn, providing one-word answers to your questions, not initiating conversations, and you ask, "What's wrong?" and he or she says, "Nothing." Which communication do you believe, the spoken word or the way of being?

The same is true for you. If you gossip about your employees (gossip is when you speak about people when they are not there in a way that diminishes them to others), then do not be surprised when they gossip, because your way of being is "Gossip is okay." Whatever ways of being you tolerate and justify for yourself will show up around you in others.

Your access to changing others' behavior is to first go within and alter your way of being. Inquire within yourself, "Where do I do that and think it is OK?" Become aware of where you "be" that way and make a commitment to be different in the future.

Being the change is a process of growth and development. It requires that you have compassion for yourself and others, that you acknowledge your influence on your world, and that you have a willingness to let go of blaming others for the way things are.

Go ahead...be the change!

Insight: _____
_____
_____
_____
_____
_____
_____

What this means to me is: _____
_____
_____
_____
_____
_____

Ideas for Action

The boldest action I could take regarding this insight is: _____
_____
_____
_____
_____
_____

The action I am committing to is: _____
_____
_____
_____
_____
_____

About the Author

Lisa Giruzzi has more than twenty-five years' experience helping people be more successful through effective communication. She specializes in assisting organizations to empower and engage their employees to be successful and productive by training managers and supervisors in the principles of effective communication and performance. She has discovered the key elements necessary to ignite and sustain positive change and has developed a revolutionary program to train others to do the same.

Lisa began her career in the field of social work, primarily assisting families in distress. During those difficult times, effective communication was essential to create successful outcomes in very emotionally challenging situations. Her experience as a social worker left her with one profound lesson: the key to being successful in any situation in life was her ability to communicate. From that time, she made it her mission to learn everything she could about effective communication and its impact on one's ability to produce results. Since 2003, Lisa has focused her mission on causing positive, sustainable change in the workplace. Her unique approach has helped numerous organizations, both public and private, achieve their goals.

She is the author of *31 Days to Transform Your Life* and co-author of *42 Rules for Creating WE*, which Angela Ahrendts, chief executive officer of Burberry, called "today's greatest guide for team success." The book reached number one on Amazon.com in the Leadership, Management, Motivation, and Organizational Behavior category and was an overall best-seller. Lisa has co-authored articles on appreciative leadership that have appeared in *Leadership Excellence Magazine* (a Warren Bennis publication). Her newest book is titled *Bringing Out the Best in Your Employees: The Ultimate Guide for Managers and Supervisors to Engage and Empower Employees to Be More Successful and Productive through Effective Communication*. She is a co-host of the television talk show *Real Conversations* and is a dynamic speaker, captivating audiences with her powerful message at keynotes, presentations, and workshops nationwide.

Lisa is the owner of the consulting firm Transformational Conversations, specializing in communication and performance; a founding member of **The Creating WE™ Institute**, an international group of critical thinkers dedicated to harvesting new forms of engagement and communication in the workplace; and co-owner of **Appreciative Inquiry Consulting**, a consortium of consultants dedicated to creating a positive revolution in change using appreciative inquiry.

Lisa lives in Albany, New York, with her husband, Bill, and their adorable Maltese, Toby.

Made in the USA
Charleston, SC
12 June 2011